Pourings of Love

By
Samantha Hurst

Reviews

I just finished reading "Pourings of Love". It truly is an outpouring of love. I love how the love that pours out is one that embraces all of life. Its words coalesce into an ever-shifting dance that helps us get a greater glimpse into what true love is. This dance is both personal and universal. It is perfectly flawed by our humanness and it is eloquently formed out of our divinity. There is so little out there that points people to this kind of all-encompassing love. Very little speaks of love as the very source and substance of all that is. Very little recognises the very foundation of life as being a single dance of love into all the varieties of human experience, even our loss and suffering. And I love how the insights into this bigger love keeps on bringing us back to experience being "heart-broken-open" to an unconditional embrace of the whole of life.
May your words spread far and wide and touch souls and awaken hearts!

Dr Dicken Bettinger - Psychologist and Author of Coming Home

Samanthas poetry has the tender fullness of Mary Oliver's writing and the stark honesty of Khalil Gibran's. But is of course unique to the beautiful essence of Samantha Hurst. It is powerful, unpretentious, raw, sublime, honest and transcendent. Each word is to be savoured.

Clare Dimond - Author and Teacher

I love how Pourings of Love compiles the journey from naively falling deeply in love, slowly into the destruction of heartbreak, to finally discovering the importance of loving the self as a foundation for future love. Each page is broken up perfectly, telling the story with short statements in between to give the mind some reprieve from the previous poem and to prepare for the next. This was extremely touching for me as, I'm sure like many people, my heart has been hardened as life simply takes its toll. The entire writing magically reminds me my heart truly is still soft...and for that I thank the writer. I find the entire premise and feel of this work compelling and riveting. It allows the reader to relate early and easily and to be taken by its' flow.
This is a truly beautiful piece of work.

R Banks — Movie Producer

'Pourings of Love' is the perfect representation of the savage beauty of being in love. The searing honesty with which Samantha lays her heart bare on the page stirs memories of those loves and losses that have touched our lives and left their scars. I found myself nodding with agreement through my tears as she bravely and unashamedly confessed that her heart was broken and she was not ok with it; she speaks a universal truth with a distinctly singular voice.

This book is relatable, yet deeply personal, achingly sad, yet soul-soaringly beautiful.

This book is music, and it's a song for the lovers.

Sarah Pettican — Literature Teacher

Foreward

In this book, Pourings of Love, lies a love story, a story of my love for another, for we never really know what lives in another's heart. Ultimately the love that we feel comes from within, so my story is the only story I can tell. The connections that we make are a catalyst for the love that we are and when thoughts of the self fall away we melt into another, we merge into oneness, we see beyond the illusion of separation. My story is one of someone who had thought that romantic love was a thing of the past and then one day I was caught by surprise and I fell in love. He was my catalyst and he became my desire. I now see that when you are meant to love then love will find you. There is no protection from it, we have no choice.

This beautiful experience brought to life something long forgotten within me and although ultimately he could not give me the love that I desired, it broke me down and opened up my heart and its infinite ways to love. An awakening then occurred and a deeper knowing of what true love really is. The experience also gave me the sometimes seemingly unbearable pain of a broken heart. The words that follow poured from me during this time.

I hope that they may now pour into you and touch a place within you that may need to be awakened or remind you of your beautiful divinity and the love that you are made of. As painful as this experience has been at times I am happy that my heart has been touched and that love has been set free in the long forgotten places within my soul and that from that time my story of love was born.

First edition paperback copy 2019
ISNB.No 9781710229721

Cover painting by Samantha Hurst
Cover design by @boogiecrypto

"This book is music, and it is
a song for the lovers."

Note from the author:

This year I experienced a love affair that shook the foundations of who I thought I was. During this time these words started to pour from me, forming every morning as soon as I opened my eyes. On some days I would have to pull my car over to write, the words were relentless in their pursuit of being written. The end result is this book. I now want to share these words with the world and show people that the experience of falling in love and the heartbreak that can follow should not be feared. It is a beautiful thing and even if it leads to suffering it can give us a much greater understanding of who we are and what we want from our one precious life. This has been the most beautiful and the most difficult project I have ever undertaken. The words on these pages are raw, honest and perfectly reflect my experience and my heart. Laying my vulnerabilities bare for all the world to see can be daunting at times but I know that this work wants to be seen and that its message will help others in overcoming heartbreak, healing and awakening their beautiful hearts.

"In your light I learn how to love.
In your beauty, how to make poems.
You dance inside my chest where
no-one sees you, but sometimes I do,
and that sight becomes this art."

Rumi

And from nothing the spark of life
was born

A formlessness into form

And when life sprang forth
from the seed of the formless
when stardust and
moonlight were born
there was the thought
of a me that knew
it was made
to love you

Love found its way into the
cracks of my heart
ripping it open for me to see
that my heart is not
a tiny part of me
it is eternally
infinitely
all of me
and I love
all of you

So I whispered to love take me
as if I ever really had a choice…

I fell the instant that I saw your
face and I remembered who you are

I long for the day you kiss away my
tears of desire

I want our oceans to meet
for time and space to dissolve
to drown with you
in a moment
without time
no fear
no longing
no waiting
as silence sings
the song of us
we melt
into
the
depths
of
love
never
to
surface
again

We
are
one

The wild flowers of my love
were dancing in tune
with a silent orchestra
that played your song
which gave me no choice
but to bloom
with all the colours
that you bring

I love you exactly as you are

A love lighting us up
A fire burning through us
raging from deep within our souls
coursing through our veins
filling us with desire
until nothing was left
but the you and I
that lay hidden within
shining like the brightest of
loves diamonds

What a life this is
with your hand in mine
what a life this is
melting in the divine
with each breath I am here
our lives entwined
what a life this is
a spark that shines
what a life this is
it burns so bright
what a life this is
let's dance all night

The arms of my beloved
wrapped around me
kissing me better
with soft whispers
of the truth
of who I am
moving into me
holding my ache
licking my back
in this presence
I merge with love
to feel safe again
love holding love
in loves
infinite arms

Love finds you

Formless into form

Part 1

I experience this love in the space
from which I now live
to know I am that which experience
passes through
the space of pure presence
that these feelings are not me
that I do not want or need you
yet I am you
to be at peace with life
exactly as it is
living from
the still waters
of a love
that requires
nothing
lacks
nothing

Formless into form

Part 2

And then my humanness rises
and tells me I need more
that this love can hurt me
that I should
say goodbye
before my heart breaks
and I rage at
the unfairness of it all
as the waves crash
against the shores
of my heart
they knock me down
fear grabs me
pulling me under
falling deeper
as I scream
and then I touch
the stillness within
and I know
I have no choice
but to be this love
in this moment
drowning in
my thoughts of
you

I am completely and
utterly in love
with every atom
of your being
so I surrender
and love with a
totality that is
meant only for the
brave souls who are
willing to burn
their hearts in
the fires of love

The tenderness of my heart is no longer hidden away. It feels like it has been absorbed by my skin and is touching all it sees, allowing itself to feel the light of existence and all the colours it brings. Colours so bright that they burn through the stories I use to keep myself safe. Sweet tender vulnerability full of exquisite pain, old heartbreaks and an enormity of love are present, perfect and unencumbered by all the barriers I had put against them. Expanding into all that is, knowing that I am love, we are love, without condition, infinite and forever, always mine and forever yours.

Oh how you make my heart sing the
sweetest of loves songs…..

Moonchild
Moonchild

Love freely
Love wild

Dance under the moon
As you love on this night

Let her light guide you
Feel the magic inside

Cast your desires
Catching dreams as you go

Kiss under starlight
With eyes gently closed

Moonchild
Moonchild

Do not be scared anymore
For love will guide you and carry you home

No one will hurt you
And love will be there

Waiting for you
In the moons perfect glare.

Moonchild
Moonchild
No longer alone

Dancing in moonlight
Your future unknown

Lay down with your love
in the fields of desire

Let the moon and its songs
Set your love life on fire

You whispered in my ear
my soul heard
I opened up
and you came in
tearing down my walls
laying me naked
filling me up
with a love
that bought my senses to life
and my desires ran free
along the wild path of you
I grabbed you
pulling you down with me
into the darkness of my light
touching you
licking you
savouring you
scratching your back
as you scratched my heart
until there was nothing but you
urgently taking me
slowly entering me
sliding inside
as desire met desire
and all that I could ever know
was this moment
your breath
your touch
your body
your soul
your bliss
moving
as one
with mine

You play the music of my soul with the tender words that delicately fall from your soft lips. You make my body sing songs of desire with the purposeful lingering of your hand in places where my most delicate skin is hidden. With the lightest of loves touches you make me ascend to the heavens as my being dances to the sacred music of you, and as you lay before me and we move to the melody of love, a new song is born into form and our stars collide and we shine brighter than ever before.

You slid
deep inside
my mind

The thought of you
like chemistry
touching my mind
lighting a fire
that is
scorching me
and then my
hand slips
into heaven
a sacred temple
and a burning
wet raging love is born
a storm between
my legs
caressing my spine
as my mind
wanders its
fingers
all over you
finding places
that the senses in
my mind
can taste
as the thought
of you
touches
my soul
I feel you
deep inside
breathing in me
living for a moment
as one
until a sweet release
and then
a temporary freedom
from longing
and again
I am alone
with a lingering sensation
of the you
that lives within me

I saw your face
and the pieces of me that
did not have your name
written on them
fell away
leaving nothing but you
breathing my skin
loving my bones and
breaking my heart

Desire is a strange poison
it courses through my veins
filling my senses
with a wanting
that feels like it
has control over me
it pulls me down
and licks my neck
it runs its fingers all over me
and then
I feel you
you find me
teasing me
and then
you slide your love
inside me
I close my eyes
and grip onto you
as love is transformed
into you and I
a physical merging of our desires
love takes us
we look into each other's eyes
And as you move into me
I arch my back
and my desire is released
in an ecstatic dance
to be at one with you

We are the song that the
universe sings

for now

I sacrifice myself to love
over and over again
I lay at its door
beaten by my own doing
asking it to take me
once again
into my sacred home
I know this door I lay at
but I resist its open arms
lost in my stories
of what love isn't
but then
with one breath
I melt away
I am gone
dissolving
into the love without form
beloved truth
blessed knowing
held
loved
turning away from myself
back
once again
into my sacred home

"I see that we are made of stars"
he said
"But can you see the beauty?"
"It's just a fact" he said
"But it's so glorious, look up,
it's so magical and sublime"
"Oh" he said
" I think we are from different
worlds"
"Different galaxies"
She sighed

Tread carefully
in my heart
my love
for you know not
what you do
when I think that
you are back to stay
but you say you're
only passing through

When our story ends
and this love dies in our arms
you will mourn its loss
and you will regret
that you were
never brave enough
to burn in the fire
or dance in its light
and I will too
but at least
I know I would
have tried

Today we will say goodbye
knowing that my heart
will shatter into a million pieces
within a space in which it
can never be broken
but it will feel
that way
for now

Words fall from you
and worlds fall within me
my heart shatters

You ask me how I am
a tear falls
I do not want you to see it
so I turn away
pain sears through me
my body tightens
my heart breaks
fragmenting into pieces
each one an agony
all of its own
I wipe away my tear
I turn towards you
I touch your face
for the last time
and I smile and say
I'm fine

And then you went away

and my tears began…

Rawness
splitting, breaking, stripping
me down to nothing
by consciousness revealing
all the lies i tell myself
returning to what's true
I scream in the terror of vulnerability
pulsing within the wide open space
of a true self
that knows only love
it wants to take me into its arms
but I resist
I kick in fear of something dying
crying
then a deeper known appears
of absolute nothingness
born from itself
a singing emptiness
a loss
and then I am taken
I have no choice
but to surrender and fall
into loves never ending arms
this truth
much greater than i will ever know
brings me beaten to loves doorway
I am let in
embraced
and in a moment I dissolve
to be born
to die
to know
to see
to love
to feel
and be kissed
in places
I never knew
I had

The soft spot for you
turned into a deep well
into which I fell
lying at the bottom
in the darkness
where you could not see me
but I'm not sure
you ever wanted to
you always seemed to want
to rescue anyone but me

I tried to steal the moon for you, to keep you held in its glimmering light, reflecting the love that I felt for you, hoping that you would see me.

I tried to catch the sun for you, to light you up and show you the magic that lies inside of you, just below the lies you told me to keep yourself safe.

But I settled on showing you the stardust and galaxies that lie within you, the infinite luminous love that you are beyond the stories of a you and I.

But still that wasn't enough for you.

You crept into my heart and I do not
know how to get you out

If you think the ends of the earth are as far as I would have gone for you then you are wrong. I would have sailed starships across long forgotten universes to kiss your lips, to touch your skin and to feel your breath on the back of my neck.

In the silence I can still
hear your heart whispering my
name through tears of regret

The breeze whispers your name in my
ear, it caresses my skin with your
touch, but all I want is for it to
find the place inside my mind where
you live, so it can carry you far
away from me, so I may begin
to forget just how much
I love you.

Everything
and nothing
all at once
then for a moment
no you
no I
one
bliss
this
I try to hold you
but you slip away
and then
I am alone
without
aloneness
laying
in
darkness
silently
singing
of
our
love.

Saying goodbye
to a love
that came from me
but looked like you
is still a pain
that feels
like a thousand
tiny cuts
to my
heart

You were the flower that bloomed in
my heart and the thorns that
scratched me when I tried to pick
you and keep you for myself.

I tried to catch your love in my favourite cup so I could sip you all day long but this love kept falling out and splashing me, making stains and burning my hands so I poured it away. I still wonder whose cup you are filling up now and if you are still making a mess wherever you go.

I wish I could say you left a bad
taste in my mouth but all that's
left is the taste of your sweetness
on my tongue and a burning desire
on my lips

I miss your voice most of all
the way it curled up my spine
calling my name
catching my breath
as you whispered
loves intent
softly in my ear
touching my soul
sending me down
taking you
wanting me
feeling you
in me
as your words
caressed me
touching me tenderly
softening me slowly
as the rhythm
of our love
is born
into form
once again

I wish I could erase
you from my mind
To cut you off from the start
To protect my precious heart
To not cry tears of pain
To not ever know your name
I wish you would just
love me again

I am consumed by the noise of you.

Even in your silence.

The crystal clear waters of our love became muddied by words misconstrued into meanings not meant and hearings not heard whilst everything that was true could be found in the still silent waters of our hearts

I was given the map to stop loving you
but I took a wrong turn and found
myself lost along the road, it was the
road I had once found you on but you
were no longer there and all I found
were memories of the joy that once was,
a joy that has now been drowned in
tears of sorrow from your goodbye, and
the shattered pieces of the broken cup
which you smashed that had contained
our love, without ever looking back to
see if I had slipped and lay
bleeding in the mess that
you had left behind.

I did not know where I had left you so I went to the lost and found to look for you but you were not there. Then I looked between the lines of my poems in case you had slipped and fallen into one of them but you were gone.

Some days I feel as though
I am trapped in a
cage made
with my
thoughts
of you

And when I close my
eyes I am with you

It makes me never
want to open them again

The flowers grow wild
in the garden of my dreams
weaving patterns
waiting to be seen
reaching to the sun
in soft stillness
and silky light
they shine
wanting nothing
but to exist
and hoping
to be seen
by you
once again

I still take photographs for you

I kiss you goodbye
and I wonder why
my heart still weeps
does it not listen
can it not hear
the world calling for me
with lovers falling at my feet
and sweet poetry
filling the air
yet I see the face of my beloved
in all I meet
and then I smile as
rose petal footsteps
guide me
soothe me
sing to me
on this balmy love filled
summers eve
and with a sweet touch
and a soft caress
the gentlest of
loves breezes
brushes against my skin
and as the music plays songs of you
I begin to dance
and I know that my
boundless heart
will decide
when it is ready
to let you go

In another place
In another time
In another life
I will find you first

The pain of separation feels too
real to be an illusion and
yet I know
it is

I miss you

The wild waves that crashed against the shores of my heart when you said that you loved me left me drowning, fighting to catch my breath. As I sank into the depths of life's love I prayed with all my might for that which I could not have, only to be left washed up on a lonely shore laying in the devastation of loves lost storm. As I lay there looking up at the cloudless skies I remembered the infinite nature of my beautiful heart and its love that only knows giving whilst asking for nothing in return and I cried until my tears were dried by the angels of grace and the gods of time, until once again peace washed over me and the still waters returned reminding me that I am love always and in all ways.

Life bought you to my door
Some days I wish I had not opened it

And yet still I hope

Heartbreak is
a temporary pain
revealing
an explosion
of the senses
that will bring
a new vision
to life and
its wonder filled
glorious beauty

But for now
it will make me miss you
until you become
someone I used to know
and your face fades
in my memory
and I will
say goodbye to the dream
of holding your hand
and growing old
with you

I danced through
loves door
not knowing it would
dissolve everything
I knew
leaving nothing
but a vast emptiness
full of every pain
I had forgotten
arising to be loved
then dissolving
into nothingness
meeting a
deep love
for all that is
and for a me
that thinks
it can be anything
other than enough

I want to be wrapped in blankets as soft as clouds whilst love gently kisses my heart better for you are no longer here and a piece of me is lost, the flowers of heartbreak grow wild in my garden, tearing my skin, watering my eyes and scratching my heart. Loves loss has made the colours that looked so bright fade to black and white and the trees are now bowing in your absence, so I will lay here in blankets of regret with tears staining my pillow until I am empty of you and the pain of loves lost tomorrows.

I awaken as
the moon waxes full
I go to touch you
you are not there
my heart remembers
that you are gone
my body feels
your loss
the break returns
to my heart
rivers fall
from my eyes
as I lay in darkness
and pray
that you never
try to love me again

And then the moon bowed down
and whispered to my heart…..

"enough now, moonchild, enough"

Today I will sing softly of our love
as my heart feels like
a tender place
where footsteps need
to be gently taken
whilst we whisper
to each other
sweet vulnerabilities
that softly stroke
my skin
I will stay here
safely hidden
until I am ready to
face this world
without you
once again

As the words pour from me
I see that they come
from the sweet hurt
that my heart
feels when
it yearns for things lost
but I know that there is too
much pain in chasing
that which is not meant for me
so I turn and face the sun
and I surrender
to the pure presence
of the now
and like a flower opening
I take the gift that
you offer
and I bloom
knowing that I am
meant for the life I have
and that all seasons
have their place
in the beauty of
my soul
and I marvel
through my tears
at the glorious
perfection
of it all

The storm of love passed
through leaving nothing
but poetry in its wake

...and you will always be
my unfinished poem

I have poured my heart out
with tears
and now it is empty
waiting to be filled
with stardust and moonbeams
on a love filled warm
summers night
where I remember who I am
and fall into the love
that will never leave
the love that I am made of
the love that shines in the
pure presence of every moment
below the thoughts
of a me that thinks it
needs a you

Today I learned that gifts do not always come in pretty packages with bows and ribbons full of sweet things and heaven scents, sometimes they come in the form of people that break your heart. But these people may have shown you how to love again and to touch the tender places that have remained hidden for so long. When these precious gifts come please cry your beautiful heart out, lament in the sadness that you feel but know that you have been broken open to love more deeply and to feel more tenderly and to know that love is not only something you receive but it is what you are made of and may you always remember that you can only be and will always be enough.

I awoke and
opened my eyes from
the slumber of my humanity
and I rose from
the pain
that was not
caused by you
but by a me that believed
in an imaginary future
in an imaginary life
where I longed for you
to be with me
a me that
needs nothing but
this moment
and it's pure perfection
a dazzling luminosity
a deep glimmering
presence
a glimpse of truth
into our infinite
existence
and the wisdom
to know
that even your
absence is
the most perfect
gift of love
that I ever
could receive

As the storm wained
I peaked out from under my
blanket of insecurity
and a sense of peace
came over me
a knowing that
this moment could not be
anything other
than it was
that you could not be mine
that I could be nothing other than
enough
that I would carry on alone
and love would
take me home
and kiss my heart better
and help me forget
the love that
could have been

You have softened the edges
I had used to protect me
that had been forged
from past hurts
and pains that I thought
I could not bear
the gentle me
that has emerged
from the fire of your love
thanks you
for this gift
a gift of love
that I will share with the world
that you will never
know you have given me
but I will
and I shall hold it gently in my
heart
and I will remember you sometimes
as I smile
and look to the stars
and wonder….

Somewhere our souls
are dancing together
in stunning moonlight
naked
dressed only in the
jewels of love
shining for all to see
no longer hidden away
in a love
that cannot be
but wild and free
lost in the bliss
we know
lay hidden
waiting to be
revealed
by loves light
and then the planets will rejoice
that love has found its way
and the heavens will sing
the song of us
and we will lay in
each others arms
and warm ourselves on
the burning fires
of desire
and as day breaks
all the universes
will be singing
stories of our love

And the fairytale in my mind was washed away, like a sand castle that was ready for the waves of destruction to clear away all hope, ready for a new dream to be born from the sands of time and the waves of my soul. I sat in the knowing that I would bathe in the moonlight once again and that someone new would touch my heart and fill me with songs of love once more.

I choose to let life carry me, to let it have its way with me. I can fight the tide no more and so I flow, I let go, I surrender to the moment exactly as it is. I let life carry me into the unknown as you slip away like water on my skin, I shine on and live this gift of life that I have been given and I bathe in all the boundless beauty that it brings

Today my heart yearns for foreign lands where my painted feet will touch new ground and the bells on my ankles will ring in smiles and laughter. I will catch the eyes of those I pass and we will recognise each other's divinity and laugh at the madness of love and life, I will swirl and dance as one with all I meet as the sun tans my soft skin and reminds me that I am the essence of life itself, reminds me that I am love and that love can never truly be lost.

And in one tiny glimpse
the magic returned
life bowed down at her feet
and laid the path
with jewels and stardust
beckoning her forward
as she threw her head back
and laughed at the
utter perfection
of it all.

nothing was ever really lost
nothing can ever truly be found
there is just an unfolding
a coming together
a falling apart
creation
destruction
both are beautiful
when seen from the singular
when we know
that nothing in this world
was ever truly ours anyway

my heart and its secrets
it will never tell
the pain that it bears
the joys it has felt
the loves that have scratched it
and torn it apart
the beauty and wonder
of my precious heart
that carries on loving
regardless of pain
that will love you forever
even though it's in vain
for this heart without condition
knows only one thing
to sing songs of love
for the joy that they bring
so others may hear
when they suffer and scream
that love keeps on loving
no matter how dark it may seem

My love for this splendorous life knows no bounds, even when my feet are torn and scratched from the lessons I have learned and the paths I have trodden, I still marvel at all the colours that it brings. Each footstep I take is perfectly placed by loves grace. So I kneel, I bow down to the love that lay hidden behind every door for now I know that there is nothing that can stop this divine love that pours from me. For in truth I see that I am love and love is me, a love that can only and ever be wild and free.

The path is wild
do not tame it
with thoughts
of how it
should be
keep it unkempt
and dance along it
sometimes it will
scratch your feet
and graze your knees
its nettles may find your
heart and sting it
but you know you
will have lived
from the scars
you collect
and the flowers
that you pick
that you wear behind your ears
tucked into
golden locks of hair
shining in rays of
love and sunlight
and you will not look back
as the untrodden path
will call you on
to find treasures that you did
not know existed
waiting for you
to see
them and
notice life's
infinite joys
once again

"You may try a hundred things, but love alone will release you from yourself. So never flee from love — not even from love in an earthly guise — for it is a preparation for the supreme truth"

Jâmî

Epilogue

When you experience a love like this it should make you question everything. It has come to shake your foundations. I think DH Lawrence said "falling in love is a catastrophe" and it is, it takes you over, it heightens the senses, it makes you crazy, it keeps you up at night but it is also heavenly and divine. It makes you feel alive. It breaks you wide open revealing more of who you truly are. So when love does comes along, when you feel so hopelessly in love you think you may break, do not close down, open more, see more, love more. This love is showing you what you are made of, it is calling you home. Feel all of it, the joy, the madness, the pain, the desire, for our humanness is a gateway to our divinity and you are divine, so divine, so perfect and I hope that somewhere in these pages you have had a glimpse of that and that you have seen the beauty that you are and know that if you find yourself lost in loves suffering these words have come to hold your hand, comfort you and bring you home again.

Here lay the
Pourings of love
Spilling from my heart
Telling my truths
And exposing
My sweet tender
vulnerabilities

With love
Samantha

Samantha Hurst is a writer, artist and coach.
To find out more about her please go to
www.artistcoach.org

Thanku2….

Everything I do is for my son Hari. He is the love of my life and the person that taught me unconditional love on the day he was born into this world.

My mother for her unwavering love and support throughout all of life's trials. I love you more than any words.

To all my lovely family and friends but especially Emma Taylor, LD, Mr Banks, The Core Gang, Dr Dicken Bettinger, The GF, Boogiecrypto, Clare Dimond, Sarah Pettican, and everyone who donated to my Kickstarter Campaign, you made this possible. Also a huge thank you to my Twitter Family for your constant support and to you the reader for taking the time to buy and read this book. I have pourings of love for each and every one of you.

Samantha

Printed in Great Britain
by Amazon

33880611R00111